Castle of Shadows

By: Jesse VanDyke

Ever wonder, like David, if you have bravery inside?

... Just Wait.

For:

My father, Roger, thank you for the times you spent reading my brothers and I stories in our bunk bed.

My wife Joy, thank you for always encouraging me to follow my dreams, and

My son, Tristan, I hope you grow up to be a man of courage.

New Castle Publishing

Lake Worth, FL

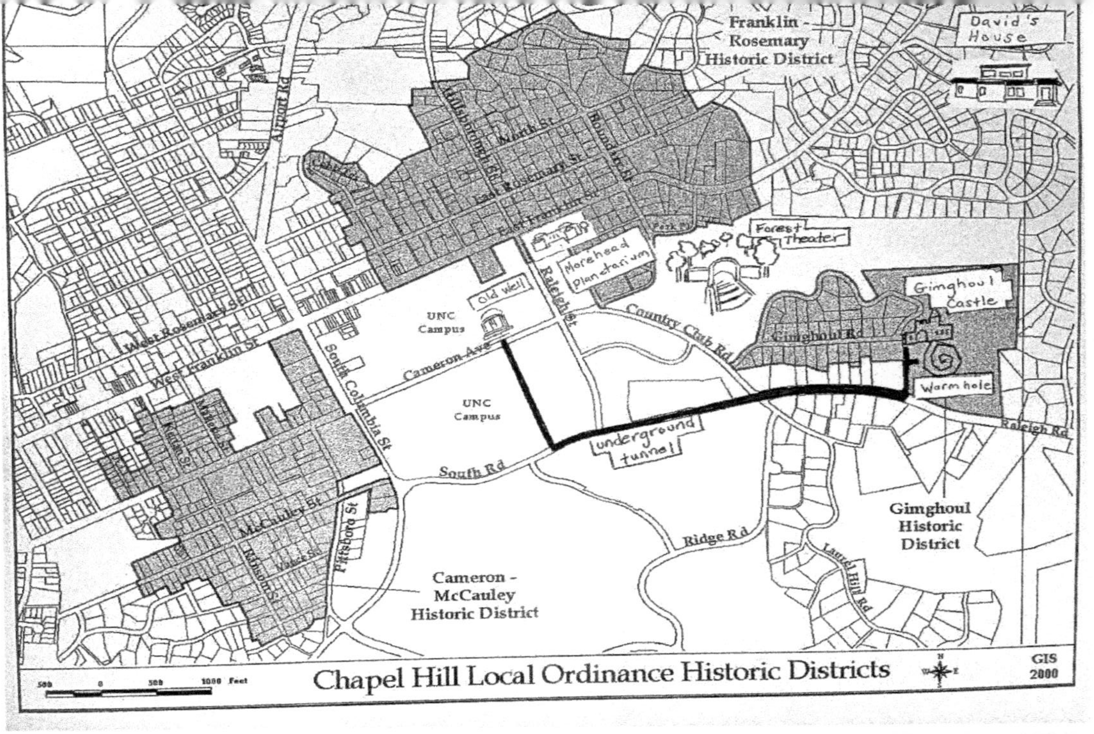
Franklin - Rosemary Historic District
David's House
Airport Rd
Hillsborough St
North St
Boundary St
East Rosemary St
East Franklin St
Forest Theater
Morehead planetarium
Old Well
Raleigh St
UNC Campus
UNC Campus
Country Club Rd
Gimghoul Rd
Gimghoul Castle
Warm hole
Raleigh Rd
West Rosemary St
West Franklin St
Cameron Ave
South Columbia St
underground tunnel
South Rd
Kenan St
Mallette St
McCauley St
Pittsboro St
Ransom St
Vance St
Ridge Rd
Laurel Hill Rd
Gimghoul Historic District
Cameron - McCauley Historic District
Chapel Hill Local Ordinance Historic Districts
500 0 500 1000 Feet
GIS 2000

"At the eastern edge of Chapel Hill,

Tucked away among the trees, lies an ancient castle,

Behind it, sprawls a high wooded cliff lined with stones,

The view from it is beautiful.

A dark, clouded shadow spreads across the earth, covers the trees and whispers evil in the wind..."

Chapter One- Trouble at School

Looking sideways at his shadow, on the cracked gravel, concrete schoolyard, a boy rises from his back after being shoved backwards over a crouched student.

"You're such a coward, David," yelled a scowling classmate as he walked away.

"Next time you'll think twice before sticking your nose in our business," remarked another. David Wesley, a medium-sized, dirty blond thirteen year old was used to being picked on. He'd spent most of his seventh grade year just trying to get by unscathed. Switching schools frequently, he was often labeled as the new kid and found it difficult to make new friends. He also had little restraint, speaking his mind to stand up to bullies. That usually got him into trouble, especially because he didn't have the courage to physically challenge anyone. David sighed and brushed the dirt from his jeans. He glanced over at a younger boy, who had slicked hair and glasses. With a slight smile, David nodded in his direction, then grimaced, touching a scrape on the back of his neck. He wished that doing the right thing felt a little less painful.

Meanwhile, in the distance, just beyond the tree line of the schoolyard, silently observed a dark, shadowy figure, watching...waiting…

Leaning his head back on his pillow of the top bunk, David was careful to watch the bandage on his neck. He pulled the sheets up to his chest. The door opened and

David's father, Jack Wesley, a man in his early forties, stood there with blue eyes that wrinkled on the sides as he smiled.

"How you doing?" He approached the bed and stooped to pull a chair over.

"Ok, I guess."

"Listen, I think what you did today was pretty brave."

"Dad, I was made a fool of in front of my friends."

"I know David, but you stood up to those bullies to help somebody else…I'm proud of you son."

"Whatever, Thanks Dad!" David remarked rolling his eyes. Mr. Wesley smiled and pulled out a folded paper from his pocket.

"Maybe we should try to take your mind off of this. Do you remember that castle we saw awhile back near UNC campus?" David nodded. "It says here this castle was built by a secret society. The group was started around a local legend, a student by the name of Peter Dromgoole. They found his body with a bullet in his chest. He must have been important, because they named themselves after him; called their group the order of Dromgoole. They later changed the name to the order of Gimghoul, must have sounded more secret, ominous or something. They had the castle built in 1924, at a cost of $50,000, and that was a lot of money back then. Take a look at this picture of Peter Dromgoole next to the old well."

He appeared as a man in his early twenties, short brown hair, slight beard, dark, wool buttoned jacket. He leaned on the well and looked into the camera with a straight gaze, and chiseled jaw.

"Looks a little mean," remarked David.

"Just the way they took pictures back then," said Mr. Wesley.

"You say he was murdered?"

"Yeah, in a pistol duel. The article says in 1833, Peter was killed for his love, a woman named Fantine. The weird part is that after Peter's death, nobody ever saw Fantine again, not her parents, her friends or Peter's murderer. She just disappeared."

"Probably wanted to run away from her problems," said David, "I know the feeling."

"It's only a legend David, hard to tell the truth from the story. You should probably get some sleep, it's gettin' late." Mr. Wesley stood up and ruffled his son's hair. He whispered goodnight and flipped off the bedroom light, and pulled the door closed behind him.

"Wait Dad?"

"Yes son?"

"Could you leave the door cracked with the light on in the hall?"

"Sure will, sleep tight."

David yawned and lay still in his bed. He allowed himself to be lulled by listening to the rhythmic sounds of the outside crickets. It wasn't long before he dozed. Not long after, he was startled awake by the nearby sound of thunder. In the darkness, he quietly listened as raindrops pitter-pattered on the roof and windowpanes. The clock blinked 9:47 over and over again.

Power must have flickered.

The rain fell harder as thunder clapped startling him wide-awake. He watched as twisted, gnarled shadows danced around his room from the trees moving in the wind. His imagination pictured awful creatures of every kind in the patterns. The light in the hallway went black. David's eyes darted around the room from the hall, to the clock, to the closet and the piano. He listened as a branch nearest his window slowly scraped up and down the glass like a nail on a chalkboard. He starred, in panic, as one of the larger shadows lurked closer, blocking the trees and filling his window. He heard a faint metallic tapping on the glass, then, nothing. Only the sounds of the thunderstorm for what seemed like an eternity.

Was that the branch again?

David held his breath and without moving a muscle, he waited. Tap… scrape, Tap, Tap, Tap! It was louder this time!

David reached to pull back the covers. He slid from his bed to the floor, laying flat on his stomach. In a slow, deliberate crawl, he placed elbow after elbow to creep to the window. He placed his back next to the window, and touched the plastic window shade pull-string, which was swaying. TAP, TAP, TAP, TAP, TAP! Quick as a flash, David yanked the chord, violently opening the blinds to discover the source of the noise. Nothing! Through the darkness, all David could see was rain falling in sheets, streaking the outside glass.

He could make out the closest tree with its branches swaying in the storm. Lightning flashed! David screamed and fell back on his hands! For outside, standing directly in front of him, soaked in rain and peering into his bedroom window was Peter…Peter Dromgoole!

Chapter Two- Peter's story

August 15, 1833, Chapel Hill, NC. Peter Dromgoole stepped off his horse giving him at pat. He tied the reins to a post of a wooden gazebo. Pulling out a bucket of water from an old well, he dipped his cup and took a long, cool drink. Peter took off his wide brimmed hat and wiped the sweat off his forehead with the back of his wool jacket sleeve.

He took a moment to survey the canopy of trees that were swaying above him. The first couple autumn leaves drifted in spirals to the earth. Several students wove their way around like ants, following dirt walking paths through the wooded area. Peter brought the bucket up to his horse for a drink.

"Hey there stranger, you must be new here in town." Peter turned to see a smiling woman. She had strikingly beautiful features. Her blonde hair was held on top of her head, with several waves framing her face, blowing in the breeze. With one hand she brushed the hair from her eyes, the other was at her shoulder, holding a parasol, or sun-umbrella.

She twisted slightly, allowing her dress to sway around her feet. Accidentally dropping the bucket, Peter tried to recover by placing it back to put to his horse's mouth and act as if nothing happened.

"New in town…why do you say that?" Peter asked, slightly embarrassed.

"'Cause you're waterin' your horse with that there well. Everyone 'round here knows that horses are watered up yonder near the post office," she explained.

"Oh…sorry, my mistake. I just arrived from Virginia."

"Guess it's my duty to help a lost stranger today, lucky for me, he's pretty handsome."

"Ma'am you don't need to take me to the post office."

"Nonsense, I need a few stamps anyway, just follow me, alright?"

"Alright."

Peter set the bucket back on the base of the well, untied his horse and strolled alongside the woman.

"So…where are you from in Virginia?" asked the woman.

"Outside of Richmond."

"And what brings you to Chapel Hill?"

"I had my dreams set on practicing medicine, University of North Carolina has a great program…How about you?"

"Well, I was born and raised right here in town. My daddy works at the bank right down the road here."

"You ever thought about going to college here?"

"You are new. Colleges are for boys, haven't you heard? Women should know their place at home," she said sarcastically. "My daddy did hire me a tutor. I can read, write and even solve some arithmetic."

They arrived at a dirt road lined with shops on both sides and waited, as a horse-drawn coach with a young couple passed. Up and down the road were riders on horseback. Peter glanced at a street sign labeled Franklin over top.

Peter, his horse and the woman crossed together. The woman lifted her dress to avoid dragging it through the wet and dirty street.

"Well, I do believe we've arrived at our destination."

"Thanks …say, I never did catch your name."

"I'm Miss Mary-Jane Fanny, but I prefer Fantine and all my friends call me that. Sounds more cultured and less hillbilly."

"I'm Peter Dromgoole." She smiled and wrinkled her nose.

"And I thought my last name was bad."

"Yeah, thanks, your looking at someone nicknamed Peter Dumbgirl, all the way through primary school."

"Well Mr. Dumbgirl, it's been quite a pleasure…hope we might meet again soon." Peter stood as she stepped towards the road. She lifted her parasol and seconds later a carriage stopped. The driver stepped down to help her to her seat and away she went. Peter tied his already drinking horse to the water trough outside. He couldn't help himself from glancing back at the disappearing Fantine. This was the start of some of the best days of Peter's life.

"Seven!…" Counted the man with the gun. This had to be the worst day of Peter's life. Balancing on the edge of a cliff behind Gimghoul, with his back against a man who would kill him to get to Fantine.

Vince had forced Peter to hold a pistol so they could "settle their differences like men." The winner would keep Fantine. For the last eight months, Fantine and Peter had been getting to know each other better. Peter had known for some time that he could easily spend the rest of his life with this woman.

"Eight!..." A jealous suitor, named Vince, was also pursuing Fantine. He came back to Chapel Hill after a hunting trip in Boone. Fantine went on a single date with this lunatic and apparently that was enough to convince him that they were meant to be.

Probably the only one who's gone out with the guy, Peter thought. Vince didn't take competition well. One night, Vince forced Fantine to kiss him behind the campus store. Peter heard her scream and hit him over the head with a shovel. Peter's mind raced as Vince continued counting, "Nine!" Peter loved Fantine and was willing to fight for her. He just didn't want to have to kill anyone either. His finger played with the rusty trigger on his pistol.

“Ready…ten!” Vince swirled around; his eyes glaring like the trained hunter that he was. “Where’d you go?” Peter was high-tailing it higher up the ridge, jumping rocks like a jackrabbit. He ducked behind a large stone and waited. He wasn’t a coward, but he knew that a surprise attack would be his best chance. He thought about shooting Vince in the knee. That would probably just tick him off. He quietly listened. Through the trees, he could hear what he thought to be Vince encroaching. Then, next to his left ear…cliiicchht, a gun cocked.

“Think you can run from ol’ Vince? Lift up your hands…boy!” Peter complied. “Now, throw your gun into the gully.” Peter did as he was told and uttered a silent prayer. Vince held his gun on Peter and took three steps back. “Looks like Miss Fanny Jane’s all mine.” “Peter!” Fantine appeared suddenly from the woods, sprinting full tilt, to block Vince from shooting Peter. As she tried to stop, she tripped and slid right off the edge of the cliff! Peter barely grabbed one of her arms in time. The stones along the edge began to break loose and Peter struggled to hold his footing, along with Fantine's slipping hand. Vince could only watch in horror as they both toppled in and disappeared in the fog above the fatal trees and rocks below.

Chapter Three- Night Vision

David Wesley stared outside through the window of his bedroom. He couldn't believe his eyes. How was the late Peter Dromgoole standing outside his room, in the rain and why? Peter shifted his weight. He was dressed in a dark, grey, hooded cloak that he pulled back to reveal his face. Resting on his back, was a sheathed, shiny broad sword. He rested one of his elbows on the windowpane, and studied David with a slight smile.

"Will you let me stand all night in the rain, young friend?" David hesitated and thought about calling his Dad for help.

There was something in the way Peter smiled and spoke to him that let David know that Peter meant him no harm. He lifted the latch to pull open his window. It was large enough for Peter to crawl through. Peter glanced around before grasping the window's edge and entering the bedroom. Water dripping from his cloak, Peter yanked out the piano stool and sat abruptly. He grabbed a handful of David's shirt by the shoulder and pulled him close to his face. He whispered loudly:

"We've got a lot to talk about, and not a lot of time." Peter released his grip. "First, do you know who I am?" David stuttered,

"Y-You're Peter, but you're supposed to be dead."

"Do I look dead to you?"

"No."

"Alright then. I'm here to warn you. Even now, there is an unspeakable evil coming for you."

"What do you mean?"

“They who travel through shadows are set on killing you.”

“Who are you talking about?” Peter leaned in close.

“The Rancid. They’re hunters from the dark Shadow Realm. Their leader, Rendocrim is a shape-shifter. He knows of the prophecy.”

“What prophecy? What is going on here?” Peter sighed and quickly glanced through the window outside.

“Didn’t I tell you, we have very little time?”

Not far from their window, piercing the rain and darkness, sets of blazing red eyes raced through yards and trees. They paused, sniffed and grew closer.

“Over a hundred years ago, I was nearly shot by a man who wanted the woman I loved. She ran to save me and slipped down the edge of a cliff. I tried to save her but slipped off the edge. Thought I was a goner. Imagine my surprise to find myself in a whole other world. I fell through what my friend Wickham the wizard calls a wormhole. This wormhole transported us all the way to a different time…around the thirteenth century. Unfortunately, this wasn't the thirteenth century in our world; it's a place full of darkness, another dimension entirely. This place resembled this one and shared many similarities, but it is a world shrouded in darkness, thanks to Vasilis."

"Who is Vasilis?"

"Evil in its purest form. Vasilis has controlled the Shadow realm for as long as anyone can remember. He possesses the combined strength of ten men. He has many spies and the allegiance of Rendocrim, the shape shifter, along with the Rancids. He steals from people and kills all who oppose him. He burns their homes and villages. He stole Fantine from me to prevent my journey to find you. I've been sent by Wickham the Wizard and those in the name of King Aftan as a messenger to you."

"Hold on, so say I believe everything you've just told me, where do I fit into all of this?"

"You, David, are the one. The boy set apart to set us free. You've been chosen by magic greater than all else to help King Aftan's people, and the armies who oppose Vasilis. It has long been held close that a boy would come. As the prophecy goes:

"Evil will cease, when time is creased,
And faith enters Gimghoul in a boy.
This will summon the King,
And the light will bring
All true happiness and peace."

"The Rancids will arrive any minute, David the time to decide is now, will you help us?" David spoke from his heart as he replied:

"I don't know if I can do this. I don't know if I can help you." Peter looked at David's expression and with a reassuring smile. He whispered:

"What we lack in courage, we gain with faith." He set his hand on David's shoulder. "I will protect you my young friend." David made the choice in his mind and nodded, yes. He threw on a pair of jeans and tennis shoes.

Outside there was a rustle of leaves along with a low guttural growl. Snarling fangs and glowing red eyes met their gaze as the three wolf-like creatures paced threateningly closer. In another moment, a fourth paced alongside the others. Peter instinctively drew his sword.

"They're here!" Peter rummaged in his cloak and took out two green vials, tossing one to David.

"Drink it!" He commanded. The both did as such. Instantly David's vision cleared sharply into focus like one's might putting on glasses for the first time. David could see every detail around him, every item in the closet and each trophy on the shelf. He could read the writing on these awards…every letter of every word from across the room. This would've been impossible to see, even during the day with the lights on, never mind in darkness. David watched everything around him slow in speed. The pouring sheets of raindrops drifted down slowly like diamonds.

The wolves outside had become virtual statues. It was only then that David realized that his five senses had been enhanced but due to his speed, everything else had slowed down around him. Peter nudged David with the back of his fist. "Let's go."

Peter and David moved through the window past the wolves and around the side of David's house. They splashed through puddles as they jogged their way through the yards and driveways of David's sleeping neighbors. Through the forests and streets, they traveled, toward the downtown portion of Chapel Hill. David wished he could show off his new ability to his friends at school.

"What was that stuff?"

"It's Wickham's camouflage potion. It heightens your speed and your senses, but to everybody else, you become virtually invisible."

"How long's it last?"

"Depends on how much you drink, the amount you had'll last about a half-hour."

As the two continued running, Peter looked on in amazement at the lights and buildings as they arrived on UNC campus.

"It's strange how much has changed since the 1800's, this all used to be trees."

"Say, where are we going anyway?"

"To the Morehead Planetarium to borrow a telescope," said Peter. They could see the domed roof of the building of the up ahead with the enormous telescope inside. The rain cleared as they ran through the flower garden lawn entry. David looked up to see the clouds revealing beautiful stars.

"Might be able to see Mars if were lucky." Peter breathed heavily.

"We wont be using the telescope to look up."

"Why not, where are we going to look?"

"Were going to use it to look down." David scratched his head in confusion.

Tssssstcckisssh! Peter shattered a front window with his sword and helped David climb through. David felt guilty, even if they were there for a reason. They entered a marble-floored foyer with a large information desk. Behind it was a brass plated portrait labeled: In honor of John Motley Morehead. He wondered how Mr. Morehead felt about his Planetarium being broken into.

David glanced up to see a white security camera aimed directly at him. He hoped the security staff wouldn't be able to pause or look at the footage frame-by-frame to catch their "camouflaged speed." In the corner, a near perfectly still janitor was holding a floor-waxer. David could see the rotating rags near the floor moving in slow turns. Peter walked up and unclipped a set of keys from the janitor's belt. The two jumped over a red velvet rope with a sign that read: "Employees and Registered Guests Only." Then climbed the set of stairs leading to the telescope top.

They tried six different keys before they finally finding the right one. They entered the telescope room. Finding the place deserted, Peter sat next to an extremely large telescope. After pressing a few keys, the telescope rotated downwardly. The flat screens viewers in the front of the room flickered on. And there it was! Gimghoul Castle. Tall, majestic, it's grey rock exterior was lit up like a Christmas ornament! Floodlights illuminated its tall spires. As David focused, he noticed that the castle was surrounded by wolf rancids. He counted at least twenty scattered around the yard, two or three looked like they were tearing apart someone's cat. Mesmerized by the creatures, the sound of Peter's voice startled David.

"We'll need to avoid the castle-side entrance to the worm-hole, but there's another way. An unknown tunnel exists," said Peter, looking at a map of the campus on the wall. David watched as a picture of UNC's old well appeared on the viewers. Its appearance had changed dramatically since Peter had tried to water down his horse back in the 1830's. The well no longer looked like a wooden gazebo. Today it was a clean, white columned dome with light blue accents. This was a popular landmark around campus and a place that marked itself near the center.

"There's a tunnel here?" David asked in shock.

"How do you know this?" Peter smiled.

"Because David, I helped build it." David couldn't help but laugh. "I've been hiding in a forest stronghold with Wickham the wizard, Jenson, captain of the Aftanite army, among others. Here is that location which you can see in your world." David starred, speechless. There was a large open area covered by a rock wall on all sides. There were stone steps leading down to the base.

"You're kidding me." David recognized the location as a place he had played as a boy. "That's the forest theater…that's your stronghold?"

"You'll find it looks quite different in our world. There are pieces of our world that exist in yours. There's a connection, centering around the wormhole. Some of these commonalities include: Gimghoul Castle, The Forest Theater, and the rock walls that surround much of UNC's campus. We constructed a hidden tunnel that leads from the old well, to just beyond the castle to the wormhole cliff. This allowed me to slip by the dark army and Rancids unnoticed."

"Pretty cool," David said with a smile. Peter grabbed the set of keys from the counter and slid down the ladder from the telescope.

"Let's go!" They raced out, locked the door, but left the telescope pointed and switched on. The two jumped down the stairs two at a time, back to the marble floored entrance where the janitor still stood in the same corner. David took the keys from Peter, walked up and clipped them back to the man's belt.

"There," said David, "He'll never know they were gone!" As the two ran outside and started back toward the old well, the janitor moved. He touched the set of keys with his fingers, shook them gently, jingling them in his hands. He switched off the waxer and started up the stairs, toward the telescope room. His eyes glowed a fiery red.

Chapter Four- Underground Tunnel

As the two exited the planetarium, David felt a little sick, almost queasy.

"Why do I feel so terrible?"

"It's the after effects of the potion, it must be wearing out." David looked left and observed a newspaper frozen in mid-air hovering above the ground. It moved, increased in speed and blew normally right in front of him. His perfect vision was reduced to a closer, dimmer sight. David could only guess what lay beyond his darkened range in the shadows. He felt fear creep back in his mind as he thought of the wolf-monsters that could be tracking him even at this very moment. Now he was vulnerable.

Arriving at the Old Well, Peter reached in his pack to pull out a gear-shaped rock.

"What's that?" asked David.

"A key," Peter replied. He walked behind the fountain and inserted the key in a specific indentation in the concrete base. The indentation was so slight that even if you had visited there repeatedly you may never have noticed. Peter pushed down using his strength. The ground around the key crumbled inwardly. Holding the handle as the focal point, Peter spun it in a circle, gritting his teeth.

David stepped backward as he felt the ground vibrate under his feet. He watched the water fountain slide back, revealing a narrow hole leading straight down, like a dragon's throat. David inspected the opening to discover a ladder.

"Would you like to go in first?" asked Peter.

"Uh, be my guest." Peter flipped the stone cut key into his leather side-pack. David dropped a rock down the shaft to get a feel for the distance. Meanwhile Peter broke a branch from a nearby tree and tore a strip from his cloak. He wrapped the strip around the branch tightly in a knot. When finished, he wedged the branch in the back of his belt and carefully climbed hand-over-hand to the bottom. Once there, retrieved and cracked two flint rocks together from his pack to ignite the makeshift torch.

Cautiously, David followed him down the ladder. His last step off the rung ended with a surprise as his leg dropped into water, soaking both David's shoes and his jeans. The tunnel was knee-deep with dirty storm runoff! Together the two waded through the dark and smelly tunnel.

"Whoa…Peter!!!" Exclaimed David.
"What is it?"

"Something's in the water, it just wrapped around my left leg!"

"Don't move!" Slowly, Peter brought his torch to David, brushing his torch alongside his leg. A slippery water moccasin screeched and writhed away from the falling torch embers. Peter gave David a pat on the back.

"Don't worry, champ, jus' a water snake.

"Swell!" David shook his head.

David longed for the safety of his comfortable bed. Nearly a quarter-mile later, they reached the opposite ladder leading to the base of the cliff, behind Gimghoul.

As they climbed out, the refreshing sights, sounds and smells of the forest welcomed them. The sun was not far from rising above the trees. David sensed mystery and magic around this place. Peter yawned and stretched; standing at the cliff's edge to take in the beautiful scenery. He reached in his pack, to pull out a canteen, and accidentally dropped his tunnel key. It dropped and bounced off the rocks, wedging itself on a root about twenty feet down. The climb to retrieve it would take skill.

"I'll be back, I've gotta get that key. We can't open the tunnel in the Shadow Realm without it." David nodded. Peter tied a length of rope to a sturdy oak near the rim. He tossed it out allowing it to fall near the key. He leaned back over the mouth of the cliff, in an experienced repeller-fashion. Kicking off the rocks, he loosened his grip to glide downward. David hadn't even noticed the man approach him from behind.

"What are you doing here young man?" A university policeman shined a flashlight in his face. David stammered:

"I was just uh…camping… with my uh…cousin. Yeah, that's him down there on the rope."

"I see," said the cop a raising an eyebrow. "You have any identification?"

“Sorry officer, I don’t, I left my ID card at home.”

“How about spider-man down there, does he have any ID?”

“Not sure, he might,” David said, with a shrug.

“You live around here?”

“I live over on New Castle in the Oaks.”

“I’m on patrol because the station’s been getting calls about some vandalism and mischief. We heard about a break-in at the planetarium. We’ve also had reports of rabid dogs on the loose. A woman complained something ran away with her cat!”

“Sounds awful,” David faked as if he had heard the news for the first time. The cop’s expression softened.

“You guys just be safe out here, ok? I’d hate to see anything bad happen to ya…Uhhfff!” David felt a gust of wind from beside him and looked over to see the police officer falling forward from being clocked in the head with a metal cleaning bucket. Standing behind him was...the janitor! The cop fell to the ground out cold. The janitor shifted his form to match the cop's body type and uniform. Next, it took a thin whistle from around its neck and blew a silent puff. In the distance, wild howls could be heard responding and running toward the whistle! David called for help! The creature held him in the air, his legs swinging wildly. The creature mimicked the cop's words in a similar voice.

"Hate to see anything bad happen to ya!"

One well-placed kick to the creature's stomach was all it took. David took a breath; his heart was pounding! It took several steps back to regain its balance. Just in time, Peter crawled back up from the cliff and grabbed a huge handful of gravel and rocks. The creature saw Peter and started transform.

“Take that Rendocrim!” Peter yelled, hurling the handful into the shape-shifter. They served by bumping together, keeping Rendocrim’s form more or less intact. It wouldn’t stop him forever. Peter wrapped his repelling rope around the monster repeatedly and tied it up tight. In shock, David watched the first snarling wolf rancid approach from the forest, no more than 150 yards away. Several more were right behind. In seconds they would be upon them.

“David, jump!”

“What, are you crazy?”

“Now!”

David got a running start and leapt as far out from the edge as he could. The snarling wolves bit at Peter’s heels, as he jumped in after. The wolves instinctively stopped short from the edge and backed away.

As David fell, he felt like a spiraling kite being tossed in a whirlpool. He opened his body and the flowing air slowed his decent. He watched the seasons change and the trees shrink in size as the years crept backward. He felt the pressure of his body being pulled back in time. Then something terrible happened, the world shriveled up, and the forest erupted in flames. He exited the wormhole abruptly into darkness and was plopped on his back.

He lay on a soft blanket of something on the ground. His last thought before passing out was, ***"What in the world have I gotten myself into now?"***

When David awoke he was choking. He lay on a forest bed of thick, gray colored ash. He didn't know if he'd been lying there two minutes, two hours or two days. The smell was what he noticed first. Breathing through his nose stung his nostrils and through his mouth made him want to cough. There was a smoky haze lingering all around. He opened his eyes and thought it must have been at quite a few hours because it was so little light left outside. He stared straight up at the rocky cliff where he had just jumped. The sky had an inky blackness without so much of a speck of light from the moon or even a star. The trees were leafless, empty and bare, the limbs were mostly charred. With little blockage from the trees, a cold, icy wind ripped through the woods, like the middle of winter. The area was filled with dark grays and dull browns. David shivered and wrapped his arms around himself. There was not a sound coming from the forest that was alive not long ago. Peter stood over him, offered his hand to help David up and to his feet. "Welcome to the Shadow Realm."

Chapter Five- The Shadow Realm

"Thanks for warning me about the fall, Peter, I think I about wet my pants. What is it with this place? I can't breathe!"

"Welcome to our world, the Shadow Realm. It's cold, but don't expect any snow. It is a world that has been burned with fire and with hate. With its smoky atmosphere, the days are dimly lit and the nights are blackened soot. Ashes fall and cover the ground from large volcanic eruptions and burning forest fires. The world is neither living nor inviting. The last hope for Aftanites lies on the faith of a boy, you

David, helping spur the return of the King Aftan's kingdom."

David looked back up the cliff where they had fallen.

"How will I ever get home?"

"As far as I know, the wormhole can bring you back. We just have to make sure you jump from the right height. The higher the jump, the farther you move in time. To go back in time, jump in with your feet. If you want to head to the future, dive in headfirst!

"So, that shape-shifter and those Rancids back there will be able to follow us?" David asked.

"Most definitely," said Peter, "Which is why we should get going."

David found it hard to run, breathing the smoke-filled air. They jogged their way up and around the cliff and sneaked around to glance a Gimghoul from a nearby hill. From it, they could not only see the castle, but also a nearby ocean. This was strange to David, since in his world, Gimghoul Castle and Chapel Hill were nowhere near the coast. This castle also appeared quite different from David's time. It was heavily fortified with sentries and archers.

A drawbridge was raised and a deep moat had been dug. The castle was illuminated with blazing torches on each level. Covering the ground was an army of dark soldiers. They wore heavy chain-mail armor. Among these soldiers, were a handful of men nearly eight feet tall. They stood more than a shoulder length taller than neighboring soldiers. They carried thick swords and had the packed muscle of an ox. Their skin was pale white, and dirty.

"What's going on, what's all this?" asked David whispering to Peter.

"They're preparing for battle, they know of the prophecy. Vasilis' army has already killed many loyal Aftanites. Everyone else is tucked safely away in the forest stronghold."

For a moment more, the two watched the ruckus unfolding in front of them.

"We should go," whispered Peter.

Peter led David through the forest. He ducked over branches and around tree stumps, hacking through thick brush with his sword. David, not being used to the smoky air, became disoriented. All of a sudden, he lost sight of Peter altogether! He stood still, listening for any sounds.

"Hey! Wait up!" David yelled and his voice echoed back from a distance. It was too late. Peter had somehow disappeared from earshot. David sat down to catch his breath against a boulder. SNAP! A twig broke somewhere behind him. His heart leapt into his throat.

"Peter? Is that you?" David nervously crawled away from the noise on his hands and feet. His head bumped into something both hard and soft and his eyes rose. The hot foul smelling breath of a wolf rancid panted in his face through jagged teeth. David ran for dear life and the wolf gave chase. David wondered if anyone would hear his screams as he ran from the wolf of death.

David had no idea where he was going. All he knew was, it had to be fast. He leapt over a fallen tree and took a sharp turn to the left. The wolf cut the distance in several strides, gaining on him. What David wouldn't give for some of that camouflage super-speed potion right about now!

His foot landed on a twig that snapped, as a rope tightened unexpectedly around his leg, pulling him upside down in the air! A loud clanging bell announced his arrival to the trap-setter. The wolf creature leapt around, snapping his teeth at David's head. Three arrows shot into the wolf's mid-section from out of the darkness, killing it, instantly.

An army of soldiers unveiled themselves around David. Hanging upside down caused the blood to rush to David's head. His vision spun in circles. Meanwhile, the army drew their weapons and crossbows, aiming them at the spinning piñata that David had become.

Are these the Aftanites? David asked himself.

Peter said these guys were supposed to be the good guys!

A tall, well-armored knight approached alongside an overweight peasant. The fatter one asked:

"Who is this, Jenson?"

"He was with the wolf-rancid, Bremble, it has to be Rendocrim changing his shape. Jenson extended his right arm to aim a crossbow directly at David's head.

"Don't you worry though, before he changes again, I'll kill him!"

Chapter Six- The Forest Stronghold

David looked down the end of the crossbow aimed at his face. He tried his best to turn away, close his eyes and grit his teeth. All that was left for him to do was wait for the arrow to pierce him.

"Wait…Stop! Aftanites! Lay down your arms!"

Peter.

"The boy's with me!" Jenson released his finger from the trigger and lifted the crossbow in the air. David slowly let out a deep breath.

Peter pushed his way through the soldiers surrounding David. He grabbed the crossbow out of Jenson's hands and threw it to the ground. Peter shook his sword at Jenson.

"Don't you know who this is?!!"

"We thought he was the shape shifter."

"You were wrong. This is the chosen one, who will summon King Aftan." Peter cut the rope that was holding David upside down, which caused him to fall abruptly to the ground. Jenson took off his helmet and offered David a hand to his feet.

"My apologies, young man."

"No harm done I suppose," said David.

"We need to get to the stronghold," said Peter, "There's someone I'd like you to meet." David didn't quite feel comfortable walking through the army that had seconds before had him upside down, about to kill him. So he stayed close to Peter.

"You two better follow me," called Jenson. "The woods are full of snares I've set for protection."

The group followed behind, treading through piles of gray ash on the ground. As they continued, David noticed green leaves on the trees. A robin flew overhead and perched on a branch, powdered in ashes. The bird vibrated its body shaking the dusty mess from its feathers.

"We are somewhat protected here by Wickham's magic," said Peter. Before long, Jenson and the others moved back a layer of camouflaged trees to reveal a metal gate and stonewall surrounding the structure's outside.

"We're here," said Peter smiling. The stronghold was well camouflaged with trees and bushes planted all around the sides.

"Wickham," Peter yelled, "Let us in." With creaks and grinding gears, the gate rose, allowing them to pass underneath. An older man, wearing a long coat and walking stick, waited inside, smiling.

"Welcome back, Peter, I see you have company."

"Indeed," said Peter, grasping both Wickham's shoulders. "Come on, let's welcome our guest with a meal."

The group sat in a large dining room at a tall wooden table. All around them hung game trophies, weapons and armor. David lifted the last bite of boar to his mouth. To his right, Peter took a drink from a goblet. The group ate mostly in silence. Everyone's eyes were fixed on David. Across the table, Jenson leaned back in his chair and propped his legs up, while Bremble piled more food on his plate.

"I'm glad you both made it here safely," said Wickham. "Did you run into any unexpected trouble, Peter?"

"We had a run-in with Rendocrim and some Rancids, but we escaped."

"I'm sure we'll see 'em soon enough," spoke Jenson.

"The potion you gave us was incredible," said David.

"So, how much has Peter told you, David?" asked Wickham.

"He's told me about how Vasilis intends on destroying your people and how I'm somehow supposed to stop him."

"That's right, and soon King Aftan will return and restore peace."

"You know what I think Wickham?" said Jenson. "I think I went along with this from the beginning because I trusted the prophecy. Now, I see this little runt sitting in front of me and I'm starting to have my doubts. I've fought Vasilis' army. I know what he's capable of and I'm just supposed to trust that this boy, will somehow save us?"

"That's right," said Wickham. "You'll see."

"Does he even know what he's up against, have you told him about the tests?" David coughed.

"What tests?" He asked. Peter scooted his chair closer to explain.

"Do you remember the tunnel we took?"

"Yeah, it brought us to the worm hole."

"Yeah, well, we figured out something else. Underneath Gimghoul, we discovered underground caverns. This is where Vasilis' keeps artifacts that give him some of his power. The only problem is they're protected with dangerous traps."

"These traps are three tests," said Wickham, "each with different dangers, a test of courage, a test of strength and a test of faith.

As the prophecy goes:

"Evil will cease,

When time is creased,

And faith enters Gimghoul in a boy.

This will summon the King,

And the light it will bring

All true happiness and peace."

"This is the path that you must take, if you are meant to save us.

Of the three, faith is your final test. If passed successfully, this should summon the King."

David took a long, deep breath. Outside, David thought he heard something; he swore it sounded like men shouting.

"You hear that?" David asked. The group froze. The door burst open and Jenson stood up.

"Captain Jenson, sorry to disturb you Sir, but there is a battalion of Vasilis' soldiers approaching. We see their torch light beyond the walls." With the door open, you could hear the sound of metal armor and equipment clanking with the army closing in. Everyone rose except Bremble.

"No dessert?"

"Get my armor!" snapped Jenson. The soldier ran to obey. "You three, get a move on!" said Jenson.

"…And David?" He looked back, before exiting the room, cocking his crossbow.

"They <u>better</u> be right about you!"

David felt sick. Peter went to the wall, arming himself with a sword and shield. Wickham reached into his coat and pulled out several dark green containers. He offered them to Peter and David. The three drank and slowly faded away from Bremble's view.

Finding himself all alone for the first time made him quite nervous. He left whimpering to find a good hiding place. Bremble found a dark corner behind some crates in a back room. As he crouched in the darkness, he held his knees with his arms. He could hear soldier shouts and from where he sat, he felt the wall shake. It vibrated again and again with the impact of a battering ram repeatedly hitting the outside gate.

Chapter Seven – The Tunnel of Tests

Wickham, Peter and David exited the stronghold by a rope ladder down the backside. After descending, Wickham snapped his fingers to ignite the ladder into flames.

David observed the frozen chaos of the battle in front of him. Dozens of flaming arrows hung in the air. The dark army had spread through the forest like a plague. David waved a hand in front of an archer's face.

"Isn't there anything we can do?" David asked.

"By the time we accomplished anything of consequence, the potion would have worn off and we would be captured." Wickham said. "It is of the greatest importance that we get you underneath the castle."

"Guess you're right." He pushed the archer's body, rotating his aim from an Aftanite soldier up above the wall, towards a wolf-rancid on the ground. "There we go," David smiled.

A brisk wind swayed the trees around the old well. The absence of buildings or dormitories was surprising to David. In the Shadow Realm, the well was literally a hole in the middle of a dense forest. Peering over the edge, displayed a steep drop and a distant rippling reflection from the well floor. David was not keen on re-entering that foreboding place. Peter tied a rope to a nearby tree trunk. He first helped lower Wickham, then David, before climbing in himself. Wickham illuminated the passage with a glowing staff.

They cautiously waded further in. Instead of traveling straight across as they had before, Wickham took a left fork. This led them to a solid wall of rock, the entrance to the underground caverns, beneath Gimghoul. Peter twisted his key in a grooved lock. Gears ground, and dust billowed from the cracks. The wall plates released and slid apart, revealing a long, wooden stairwell. It led deeper into the earth, like a mineshaft. A cool, whistling draft blew a squeaking wooden sign overhead. David read it to himself as he continued down the stairs. He wondered what it meant:

Courage is letting go of fear, and walking through, when dread is near.

"From here, David, you must travel alone," said Wickham. "This is your first test of courage. Each test will reveal a gemstone that Vasilis has stolen. The gems grant great power and will equip you for what lies ahead. May God protect you." Wickham tapped his staff on the cavern floor and a soft glow spread outward over each surface. The walls, the ground, even the dripping stalactites high above glowed with a faint bluish hue.

"You can do it, I believe in you!" said Peter.

David had reached the bottom of the stairs and continued along the path apprehensively. He repeated the sign again to himself.

Letting go of fear…walking through when dread is near.

He repeated the words to himself. The cave's floor snaked in a meandering path. The bluish hue intensified to a flickering reflective orange. Was it David imagination, or had the temperature changed? He touched the walls and noticed the warmth. Turning the corner, his eyes opened wide.

A narrow passage ran through a line of hot coals before opening into a grated metal bridge that was fully engulfed in flames! David's face was drenched with sweat from heat pouring from the fire pit underneath the bridge. A small water bowl had been placed next to the start of the coals.

A small sign read:

Travelers: ***Take off your shoes and wet your feet, or burn up like a piece of meat.***

David reluctantly took off his socks and shoes. He picked up the bowl, spilling a little of the water over the lid. It plopped onto some of the coals and sizzled to steam. David dipped each foot separately into the water. David reflected on the encouraging words Peter and Wickham had said to him.

(Peter): "I believe in you."

Just for good measure he dipped his feet generously in the bowl for a second time. Lastly, he spilled the remaining contents of water over his head and shoulders. He picked up his shoes and took the first step.

His face tightened, as his feet met the coals. To his astonishment, they felt cool, moist and smooth. If David closed his eyes, he might have imagined he was crossing the rounded river rocks of a forest stream in early spring. The flames danced over the sides of the bridge where he had now come. Though flames licked across his skin, it did not burn, to the contrary, David felt the moistened chill of mist in the air. Goosebumps even formed on the back of his neck and arms.

What a peculiar experience, thought David.

Further in, he discovered a beautiful blue gemstone sitting on a small pedestal. Upon his grasp, whatever feelings of fear he had, left him completely. With the absence of the gem, a counterweight pulled a heavy door up for him to enter into the next chamber. With renewed confidence, David placed the gem in his pocket, slipped on his shoes, and walked toward the next danger.

Another wooden sign hung in view. It read:

The golden waterfall you must reach or be drowned with a silver leach.

Stooping to walk under a low bridge, David emerged observing a silver underground lake. A shimmering gold waterfall cascaded down the opposite wall, splashing into a trickling golden creek. A pedestal sat at the far end with a red ruby displayed. Feeling courageous, David stepped through the shallow end of the silver pool. Like dipping an ice cream cone in chocolate, the liquid silver coated and stuck to his legs. It hardened like iron, weighting him down and eventually pulling him in up to his chest! David envisioned the underwater statue he might very soon become. To his horror, a trap door opened, spilling more silvery waves! Up to his neck the coating continued to harden. Soon he'd be unable to move at all. In one last ditch effort, David leapt from the water to hurl his sword rock next to the trap door. Remarkably, the trap door closed, and the waves stopped. David could now take step after painful step to reach the opposite side.

He stepped under the cascading golden waterfall and allowed it to flow over his body. The silver coating melted away, allowing David to walk normally again. He picked up the red ruby. There was no change. He felt the same as he had before. He had another problem. The chamber appeared to be completely enclosed. He surveyed and found some cracks in a far wall with a giant slab against it. David wondered.

He stepped up and craned his neck to see the top of the slab. The size of it dwarfed him. He reached out his hand and wedged it in one of the cracks. As he applied pressure, the wall around it crumbled and gave way like sandstone. He crammed his other hand on the opposite side. He bent his knees and with the power of a forklift, lifted the enormous stone slab into the air. He moved backward and set it in the silver lake, causing the water to overflow the banks on either side.

Behind the rock, a moist passage led to a steep drop-off. Across the chasm was a brilliant sword, illuminated by a shaft opening to the surface. David wondered if he shouldn't try to rock climb or jump across using his new found strength. Imagining he might slip, he looked around for other options. Behind him on a jagged wall was a bat. Its legs were stuck in a silvery skeletal hard, that sat on a natural shelf.

Wonder if someone was holding on and was sucked into the silvery lake? What then happened to the rest of him? Thought David. The bat's wings flapped furiously. Above it, hung a third sign.

It read: ***Faith requires sight unseen, step with the bat or fall indeed.***

David walked forward to pick up the skeletal hand. The bat went ballistic, fluttering its wings every which way. David twisted the bat in his hands and even jumped up and down several times to see if there was any hope of some lift from the animal.

"This is insane!" He said, looking down over the edge. He found there was just no other option.

"Ok, on three," David spoke to himself, "one, two…three." He couldn't will himself to move. He remembered as a kid, he used to test the water before getting in a pool. He always thought a running-jump was better, so that way he couldn't change his mind in mid-air. He decided that this approach would work well here. He took three steps back, ran, and leapt off the cliff; worried, but not having much to do about it now. He fell a good ten feet before the bat furiously flapped its wings to miraculously lift David in the air. He glided across the chasm and landed safely on the other side. He sighed and released the bat. It returned right back to the place it came from.

"Thanks for the ride!" The sword gleamed and was uprightly inserted into a stone base. Inscribed on the hilt was the word:

"Wesley."

David grasped the sword and immediately felt warmth travel up his hand, arm and through his entire body. Light filled the room. Outside, a streak of light rose into the sky piercing the darkness. The light sucked in the smoke produced white, puffy rain clouds in its place. A gentle rain put out fires, watered the plants, and filled them with renewed life. From out of the ashes, grass grew, flowers rose and animals awoke from their slumber. The power of Vasilis was weakening.

David knelt in front of an angelic form as bright as lightning. A hand reached down to touch David's on top of the sword.

"I'm proud of you, son. Your path to me has not been easy."

"Please, is it you, King Aftan?"

"Indeed, I am."

Aftan's light faded, his short, grayish hair and whiskered beard could now be seen with his sparkling eyes. David wasn't sure if he imagined his father standing before him or if the king had momentarily changed. David remembered back in his bedroom; when his Dad, Jack had uttered the same words King Aftan just spoke,

"I'm proud of you, son." He found himself longing for home.

"This is only the beginning. I am going to lead my people, the Aftanites, to victory over Vasilis. It will happen soon. Tell my people the time for the great battle has come. If you need me yet, you have only to insert the gems of courage and strength into this sword's hilt. Remember, I'm always with you." King Aftan walked into the column of light and disappeared.

David followed through the light to find he was laying on the grass, next to the old well. Next to him, was the magnificent sword? Wickham and Peter stood above, smiling. Wickham shook David's shoulders and helped him sit up.

"You've done it my boy, I knew you could! Look at how Vasilis' power is weakening!"

"I –I saw King Afton," stammered David.

"Indeed you have," said Peter laughing.

"He told me he'd prepare an army, that we should prepare for battle.

"Then it is finally time," said Peter.

"Time to what?" asked David.

"Time to fight!"

Chapter Eight- The Trap

Minutes earlier, at the Forest Stronghold, Jenson realized he was in trouble. Though the Aftanite army had fought hard, the front gate had been broken in, unleashing a wave of wolf-rancids, soldiers and the occasional giant. Jenson, his knights and some of the commoners retreated to the surrounding upper walls. His knights continued shooting round after round of arrows into the onslaught. Jenson shouted orders to his knights.

"Ladder on the East wall! Ladder on the East Wall! Fire Men, find the giants!!!"

He noticed a small child cornered by a rancid. He grabbed a long length of rope and lassoed it around a turret. He leapt off the wall in a high arc and landed with a crushing blow on top of the wolf. Jenson scooped the boy in his arms.

"Gotcha, hold tight little one." Holding tight to the rope, his knights pulled them up together. He set the frightened boy against the rock wall, telling him to stay low.

In the distance, a bright beam of light pierced the sky, filling the forest with a blinding light. The light blinded the dark army and gave the Aftanites a decided advantage.

"Quickly, take them down!" Jenson fired his crossbow and struck a climbing soldier. They fired, reloaded and rained the arrows down. The tide of the battle was turning. Jenson smiled. Soon, he would have his victory. Suddenly, a giant's hand wrapped around his leg. It yanked him to the ground. Jenson saw himself surrounded by a group of about five soldiers. One of them stepped forward and morphed into a mirror image of Jenson.

"Rendocrim! What's the meaning of this?" Jenson's doppelganger, walked slowly around in a circle. He listened to his own voice reply,

"I'm taking care of your army. Take him away." Two soldiers grabbed his arms while another, gagged his mouth.

David was quite surprised to see the Aftanite army walking toward the old well to meet them. Peter ran ahead to meet the group. "The dark army's destroyed?" he asked.

"Yes, mostly, though some retreated and escaped. Has your group been equally successful?" asked Jenson.

“Yes we have,” said David, “I met King Aftan and he told us to attack Gimghoul. Peter looked down the dirt path, which meandered toward Gimghoul.

“They’ve got quite an army over there, we’re going to need a plan,” said Peter. They paced around thinking together. David tapped his sword on the grass.

“I might have an idea.” They walked to the old well and David grabbed the rope,

“Follow me.”

“Let’s review the plan,” Peter spoke. They all surrounded a map Peter drew in the dirt. “David,” he pointed, “You’re part one. You’ll sneak into the castle to scout Fantine’s position. Jenson and I will keep Vasilis’ army company outside to keep their attention from David. Bremble, you’ll approach the army they’ll follow you to the location of the trap.”

Bremble nodded.

"Wait, I'm the bait? What's the wizard going to do?" David put a hand on Bremble's back.

"It's an important job, Bremble, we need you." Bremble removed his hand.

"David, if I get shot, I'm coming after you!"

"May I please continue?" asked Peter.

"Please do," said Wickham.

"Once the army follows, Wickham will use his magic to hold the army in place. Then, we'll release vats of the hardening silver from the caverns. Jenson, you'll be in the tree stand, and in charge of releasing those vats to harden the army. Vasilis' army will be crippled. We'll meet David on the outside, rescue Fantine and capture Vasilis together. Any questions?"

"Yeah, me," said Bremble, "anybody have anything to eat?"

David ran at super-speed, past Vasilis' army outside Castle Gimghoul. He wore a burlap sack, stretched diagonally across his chest. He weaved through statuesque soldiers, giants, and rancids. Near the rear, there were wooden trebuchets. With his increased strength he tore them apart like toothpicks. The thought occurred that he could possibly take out the entire army himself. The words Wickham said came back to him.

"By the time we accomplished anything of consequence, the potion would have worn off and we would be captured."

He wanted to complete his mission and Vasilis posed a greater threat than his army. He shattered a window and entered the castle. He walked through a kitchen with cooks working on different stages of a meal. David popped several grapes from a clump into his mouth.

Vasilis' army scattered.

"What happened to the machines?" shouted a commander.

Appearing from the forest, a man holding a tree branch and a multicolored sheet walked toward them.

"Halt! Who goes there?!"

"It is I who obliterated your machines; I am Bremble the great and powerful! Surrender peacefully, or be destroyed!" Bremble felt the sweat pouring down his neck. His heart pounded like a drum.

David ascended a set of stairs, and passed an outside window. He glanced out and saw Bremble waving a tree branch over his head. He smiled, and then paused, momentarily feeling movement in his pack. He shifted it on his back and continued. There was a long pause as the dark soldier's assessed Bremble's validity.

"GET HIM!" shouted the commander. Bremble's eyes popped open wide. He turned around and sprinted back into the forest as fast as his weight allowed. The army followed, shooting arrows all the way.

David entered the first room on the second floor and found it empty. The second room was locked. He pried it open with his sword. Sitting in the corner and tied to the chair was Jenson! David sprung to help. He took the cloth from of his mouth.

"Jenson are you alright?"

"Yeah, Rendocrim switched places with me back at the Stronghold."
David snapped the heavy ropes like dental floss. "You've got to stop Rendocrim, he's the one who has to release the vats of silver to hold Vasilis' army."

"We've got a problem," Jenson said, looking out the window. "There's still an army out there defending the castle, how do I get to Rendocrim?"

"I've got that covered," said David, kneeling to take off his burlap sack.

"Uh, that things moving," Jenson pointed. David smiled.

"It's your ticket out of here."

Peter knelt quietly with Wickham and the Aftanite army. From where they were hidden, they would have a front row seat to the action. Strung from the trees were dozens of barrels holding the quick-hardening silver. It took the Aftanites several hours to setup of the trap. David led the group through the tunnel to the first test with coals. Jenson's knights cooled the ground with buckets from the well. Next, the army collected the silver from the next chamber. They passed them back and rinsed off in the golden waterfall. They carefully strung the barrels in the trees rigging them to dump with one chord.

Peter watched Bremble break into the forest, sprinting.

"They're coming!" shouted Bremble. He hid next to Peter and Wickham.

"Nice work, Bremble," said Peter. A group of hot, angry Rancids raced ahead. Aftanite archers picked them off one by one. Next, a spread of soldiers rushed forward, yelling loudly. Wickham the wizard held up his staff. The army froze, stopped by an invisible wall. Bremble and Peter looked to the trees to watch Jenson release the trap. Only, he didn't.

"Now Jenson!!! …Do it!...What are you doing?" yelled Peter. Jenson sat in the tree and yawned.

"I wonder how long the wizard will last before tiring!" He smiled. Peter slugged a tree branch with the blade of his sword.

"There's no way that's Jenson," he expressed to Bremble, "that's gotta be Rendocrim."

"What are we going to do?" asked Bremble. Wickham's arms began to shake in the air.

"I don't know, but I think we're in trouble," said Peter.

Chapter Nine- The Battle

David crouched in the shadows behind a large, wooden crate. He had entered a storage room; it had a loft with food supplies. David listened to voices coming from the far end.

"What do you want from me, you monster?!" David peaked from around to see a woman, being tied to a chair over bundles of hay. Looming over her was a large, dark, hulking creature. "Why are you holdin' me here?"

"To attract your precious Peter and the boy he went to find."

David sneaked around a column for a closer look. The beast lurked ominously around Fantine. The old floor emitted creaks and groans with step after weighted step. Rays of light angled down from narrow windows above. David caught brief glimpses, each moment Vasilis stepped in, then out of the light. There was a long, hooded cloak hanging over the thickest shoulders. Its bulky frame was encapsulated with reinforced armored plates. A steel helmet hid the darkness of whatever would be his face. Its eyes were piercing narrow slits of light. That occasionally fluttered and altered in color based on his emotion. David could hear the jangle of weaponry hung from his belt, the chief of which being an exceptionally wide two-handed broad sword sheathed on its back.

David shifted his weight, growing tired of crouching…creeeeaaak! His foot stepped on an old rotted board! Vasilis spun around, sword drawn!

"Come out, whoever you are." David slowly rose and bravely stepped into the light.

"Name's David, I'm here for Lady Fantine."

"You have me impressed. You're either extremely brave or just plain stupid." David drew his sword.

"Let's put that to the test."

"Cute, be with you in a minute." Vasilis turned and grabbed a torch from the wall, lighting the straw underneath a struggling Fantine. David ran forward. He dropped his shoulder and collided into Vasilis. The explosive force threw his massive body into a stack of crates, bursting them to pieces. Looking for something to extinguish the fire, David climbed the loft and grabbed a sack of yeast.

From David's perspective, everything was in slow motion. He leapt out from the loft, drifting across the length of the room. He ripped the bag open, raining white powder to quench the flames. David's feet landed with enough time to settle, just before being kicked right back out from under him. In the moment he lay on his back, he flashbacked to his school where he observed his shadow on the gravel, concrete. David looked down and noticed the shadow of Vasilis, stepping over him. David covered his face and barrel rolled to the side. A broad sword crashed down, splintering the wood floor beside his head. The creature grasped David's shirt and pulled him up to meet his iridescent eyes.

"You have no idea who you're dealing with."

Wickham was growing weaker every minute. He struggled to hold the dark army with his spell.

"Rendocrim," Peter yelled up at him, "If you've harmed Jenson in any way, I'll break you in half."

"No need for that, Peter…" a voice called from the distance. Soaring over the trees, was Jenson! His hands held tight to the fluttering bat trapped in a silvery skeletal hand! The bat banked left, swinging

Jenson's body around, to smack into Rendocrim, like a demolition ball. This knocked him all the way to the ground.

"Alright, Jenson!" Peter called. "Quick, pull the rope!" Jenson wrapped the rope several times around his arm, giving it a hard yank! The buckets tipped over, solidifying half of the army, into silver statues. The Aftanites cheered and rushed toward the remaining soldiers, retreating toward the safety of the castle. Peter helped catch Wickham, who nearly fell over from exhaustion.

"Holding that army for that long, isn't as easy as it looks," said Wickham. Peter looked over to see Rendocrim rise to his feet and regain his orientation after the fall.

"Bremble…Hold Wickham for me," said Peter. He sprinted toward the shape-shifter when something unexpected happened. Rendocrim morphed his body into a monstrous wooly beast with sharp claws and razor teeth. Peter froze with his mouth aghast. For in front of him was a creature that had grown nearly ten feet tall. What he did next was only natural for anyone facing a snarling, giant, hairy cliff monster. He stopped, blinked twice, turned slowly… and ran for his ever-dear life!

Chapter 10- Light Dawns

Inside the castle, David struggled to free himself from Vasilis' grip. Fantine was able to untie herself to swing a chair overhead at the monster. It grabbed a chair leg and pulled it away from her, thereby releasing his grip on David. By the time David reached his sword, Vasilis had a blade firmly pressed to Fantine's neck.

"Drop the sword, David!"

"Let her go!"

Vasilis hissed. "I said, put it down!" It stepped backward, applying more pressure to her neck as Fantine whimpered.

“Fine, I’ll do it, just leave her alone, don’t hurt her.” David held out a hand in show of compliance and took a step forward. It was a sideways step, his one hand placing the blade gently on the floor in front of them, while his left slipped behind carefully into his pocket.

“You know, I’ve been wondering about something. I thought maybe you could clear it up for me.” David took another step.

“Don’t come any closer!” David moved back to where he started.

“I mean, what’s your motivation, anyway? You’ve obviously read the prophecy; you know what’s coming! You know you can’t win. So the question remains, why are you still here and why go to all this trouble? Raising an army? Going to war? Kidnapping her? Why aren’t you out hiding on some island sipping drinks somewhere off the coast? Or does someone like you prefer living under ground?

“You really want to know?”

“Yeah.”

"You're right, I have read the prophecy. It hinges on a boy, lets say for now that that's presumably you. You see all of this, was orchestrated for a single purpose and now everything has been going according to my plan. See I figure, it'd be kind of hard to summon King Aftan…when you're dead!"

Vasilis flung Fantine to the side and stood poised to attack.

"You're probably right!" said David. "Too bad I already have." He took the gems from his pocket and slapped them on the hilt of his sword.

"Noooooo!" screamed Vasilis.

The sword showered light around the room as a crouched man appeared and stood to his feet. King Aftan rose and picked up David's sword from the ground and pointed it directly at him. With four words, Aftan uttered the beast's ultimate fate.

"Your time is done."

Vasilis growled and swung his sword at the King. David could feel the force as the swords collided. Clank! Cling, Clang! Scrape! The two fought their way around the room skillfully. David took the opportunity to check to see if Fantine was ok. Thankfully, she was not hurt badly. The large and imposing Vasilis repeatedly lunged at the King. David considered that despite being half the beast's size, and appearing to be an older man, Aftan fought with unmatched strength and bravery.

He deflected his attacks and used Vasilis' movements against him. Vasilis jerked forward, while the King rotated, throwing Vasilis to the ground. Vasilis got up and thrust at him again. He parried, blocking the oncoming blow. Again, the two collided their swords, up, down, and around. Vasilis threw a right hook. Aftan ducked and thrust his sword around low, stabbing him under his armored plating. Upon impact, the sword glowed intensely. Light also shot out from Vasilis' wound, from the inside. Vasilis wobbled and fell to his knees on the floor.

He writhed and shriveled into a ball of fire and ashes that fell to the ground in a pile.

"He's dead," stated Fantine.

"You are now safe and under my protection," declared King Aftan. He sheathed his sword and stepped forward. He wiped the dirt and sweat from his brow and smiled at both David and Fantine. "Shall we attend to our friends outside?" he asked. The King extended his arm. Fantine smiled and wrapped her hand around as the three walked together outside.

The Aftanites and the dark soldiers continued to battle. King Aftan raised his sword in the air. Light shot straight up in the sky, split apart like a firework and came down like a thousand arrows hitting the dark soldiers and giants. Like Vasilis, they disintegrated into piles of ashes on the front lawn, until an easterly breeze blew them away for good. The breeze continued, shoving the clouds out over the ocean. The shadows from the trees shrank until they disappeared. All that was left was what David considered to be a clear "Carolina" blue sky. The Aftanites raised their weapons and cheered!

Behind the castle, Peter's ran as fast as he could. He jumped over tree branches and roots. Pounding behind, was Rendocrim. Peter worked his way through some trees, which slowed Rendocrim down, due to his size. Peter ran along a rock-lined path, which led to a cliff. He shimmied down a lower ledge and hid. Moments later Rendocrim emerged.

"Where are you?" Peter echoed his voice off the sides of the cliff disguising his exact location:

"Why not fight fairly, or are you frightened of me?"

"Why should I, lowly Aftanite?"

"So you can brag of your victory. Then they'll write stories and songs of your great deeds." Rendocrim smiled as he thought about these things.

"And how exactly might I fight more fairly?" Peter thought for a moment.

"Change your appearance to look just like me, in size and shape, this would be the most fair." Rendocrim did as Peter asked.

"There, I've granted your request, now come out, that I might earn my reward!" Peter took a step forward into view.

"I'm here!" Rendocrim leapt over the cliff to the Peter's ledge. Peter braced his back to the wall and just as Rendocrim's feet touched the ground, Peter kicked with all his might! Rendocrim squealed, and fell headfirst into the center of the cliff. A swirling wormhole opened and sucked Rendocrim through time into the future.

Flashback. July 10th, 1833. Vince and Peter stood on the edge of a familiar stone-lined cliff, back-to-back, pistols in hand. Vince counted.

"Eight! Nine! Ready…Ten!" Vince turned around.

"Where'd you go?" Higher up the ridge, Peter listened and tried to quiet his breathing. Next to his left ear, the hammer of a pistol cocked. Cliccchet!

"Lift up your hands…boy!" Peter complied. "Throw your gun into the gully. Looks like Miss Fanny Jane's all mine!"

"Peter!" screamed Fantine, running from the woods and sliding off the cliff's edge. The stones broke loose as he tried to hold on to Fantine's hand. They both slipped and toppled into the foggy abyss. Vince stood horrified. Little did he know, but they had fallen through the wormhole and were pulled back in time to 1215, the Shadow Realm.

Vince starred down the cliff, dumbfounded. He wiped the sweat from his face and neck. He holstered his pistol and carefully climbed the side of the cliff to work his way to the bottom. He paced back and forth to search for Peter and Fantine's bodies. There was nothing.

Vince heard a loud, sonic boom and looked up in time to see the wormhole opening from the Shadow Realm and Rendocrim falling through (a Rendocrim, who looked just like Peter, I might add). He collapsed in a heap next to Vince, who silently observed. Rendocrim rose, looked up at him and growled. Vince squinted his eyes and in one smooth motion, drew his pistol and shot Rendocrim, right in the chest. Later that day, the authorities found Rendocrim's body and buried it under the name Peter Dromgoole.

Chapter Eleven- Fresh Start

An exhausted Peter climbed back up the cliff and made his way around Gimghoul, to the front yard. He stumbled up just as Jenson and the Aftanite army lifted David up on their shoulders. They clapped and chanted shouts of praise. Wickham grabbed Bremble by the arm, dancing a jig.

"You did it my boy!" cried Wickham up to David, who was high up, smiling from ear to ear.

"No, we did it!" shouted David over the noise. As Peter approached, a hush went over the crowd. King Aftan stepped forward to meet Peter for the first time. Peter knelt and introduced himself.

"Your Highness, I am Peter Dromgoole, I summoned the boy and am a loyal follower." The King smiled and stabbed his sword into the grass.

"Arise, Sir Peter, you've done quite well indeed." He turned back toward the crowd. "I believe that there is someone who'd like to see you." Peter watched as he reached back and brought forward someone's hand.

"Miss me, stranger?"

"Fantine!" Peter gasped. Peter grabbed her up in his arms and swung her feet off the ground. The crowd broke into laughter and applause.

Bremble walked over and picked up a suspicious, wooden bucket off the lawn and lifted it up to look inside. Some remaining silver liquid spilled down his neck, chest and arm, locking it in place with the bucket.

"Whoa, that's a problem. A little help here?" he exclaimed. Everyone started laughing. "Uh…Jenson…You've gotta help me, I can't move, my arm's stuck!" Jenson looked over and laughed.

"Looks like you'll have a long walk down to that golden waterfall!" Bremble blinked twice and shook his head.

"That's not funny." Still holding the bucket, he waddled his way through the group. "Wickham, you got any special potions? I'm stuck." The group laughed more and started walking towards Gimghoul Castle. Behind them was a beautiful orange sunset.

Several days later, plans had started to be carried out. The King took his throne and ruled justly and favorably towards his people, for a time. The country was renamed New Haven for it had been revitalized and was now a safe haven to loyal citizens.

Peter and Fantine were married and decided to stay in the past, as King Aftan gave Castle Gimghoul to them as a wedding gift. The King decried that a new castle be built just a little ways away. Many days later, Peter, Fantine and King Aftan joined together behind the castle cliff to say goodbye to David and send him back to his own time. Fantine bent down and gave David a kiss on the cheek, which made him blush. Peter gave him a hug and said:

"For all your help, thank you. We couldn't have done it without you my young friend." Lastly, King Aftan said goodbye. He stepped up and smiled. He ruffled David's hair and set his hand on his shoulder.

"I'll be with you David, even in your own world. I'm proud of you. You see, bravery's like a sword, you pull it out when you need it most." David nodded. He glanced back at Peter who had his arm around Fantine. David pointed down the cliff towards the wormhole.

"Look me up sometime if you ever want to…I don't know, go sky-diving or cliff jumping something!"

"Sounds good," said Peter grinning. David looked around, took a deep breath and stepped off the cliff into the wormhole.

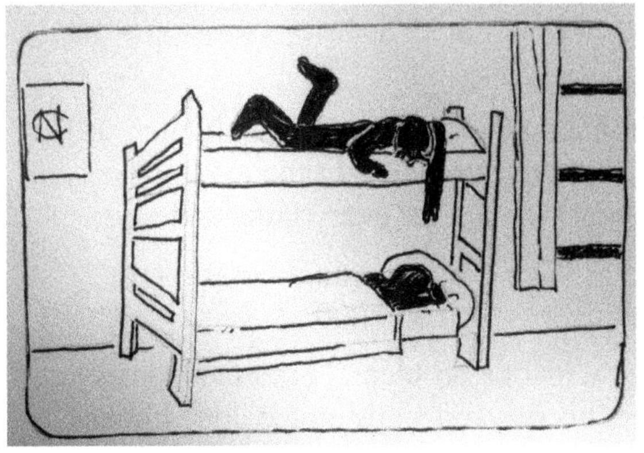

Chapter Twelve- Epilogue

Much later. Chapel Hill, 1924. A young man in his early thirties, with dark brown hair drives a companion in a rusty, Ford pick-up truck down a dirt road adjacent to cliff lined with stones. He steps out and surveys the wooded landscape around. He stops, reaches into his jacket and pulls out a property deed and a set of blueprints. He spreads them out over a large rock. He tells the builder that he has drawn up plans for a castle.

"Why a castle? What is this all for, Charlie?" the builder asks. "It's going to be donated to a fellowship, a group of friends of mine, in memory of my grandfather. It'll be called the Order of Dromgoole." The architect looks over everything, and says,

"We'll, we can do it but it'll cost nothing less than $50,000."

"Not a problem." Says the man as he takes his pen and signs on the dotted line. He traces and swoops to finish the last part of his last name…Charlie Dromgoole.

David awoke, lying back on his bunk bed. He sat up and wondered if everything had been a dream. In the darkness, he listened as raindrops started to pitter on the roof and windowpanes. There was a flash of light and a loud thunderclap. He looked at the time and saw that his clock said 9:47 pm. The light in the hallway was still on. David's dad knocked and opened the door.

"Sorry to bother you son. I heard a close thunder strike and just wanted to check in on you. You ok?" David pulled the covers up.

"Yeah, I'm good." Jack Wesley walked over and pulled up the window shades to look at the storm outside.

"Good. Remember son, tomorrow's a new day, with a brand new start." David glanced outside to notice the street sign at the bottom of his driveway, it was labeled: New Castle Place. For a minute, David imagined Peter, Fantine, Jenson and Wickham building their new castle right next to David's house! Just then, Jack shut the blinds and walked to the doorway. "Want me to leave the door cracked and the light on in the hall?"

"No thanks, I'll be ok." David's Dad turned and lifted his finger with a final thought. He stood in the doorway with the hall light spilling in.

"You see," David's Dad went on, "Courage is like an umbrella; you take it out when you need it."

David glanced back at his dad. For a moment, he thought he saw a silhouette of

King Aftan, then he blinked and saw that it was only his father.

"You know what, Dad? I think you're probably right."

"Goodnight son," Jack said warmly, as he slowly shut the door.

David lay back on his pillow. Below him he felt the bed shift just a little. He peered over the rail and smiled. He closed his eyes, relaxed his body, and drifted off, into a long, peaceful sleep.

Below David's bunk, his younger brother Ryan was fast asleep and oblivious to all...

Excerpt from Castle of Shadows 2:

There's a nondescript road that cuts and curves along a high ridge along Chapel Hill's Eastern side. If you follow it through all the way to the end...past the assortment of homes and gardens, you will find yourself looking down an aged, rock-lines forest path. The leafy branches above your head dance in the summer breeze, casting a mixture of light and shadow along the ground. If that wasn't enough, a whispering wind beacons you further in, to discover what lay just beyond your sight. It's a grand and spectacular chateau that waits, surprising to say the least. It's name is Gimghoul Castle, but behind it, an unscrupulous evil waits to be unleashed.

In this thrilling sequel, David's younger brother Ryan encounters a shape-shifting gargoyle from a world beyond Gimghoul castle's wormhole. He offers Ryan a chance to obtain his unique abilities in exchange for a small favor that will drastically change the past. David must try to somehow undo his brother's damage before time runs out. Action-packed and stock-full of humorous situations, Castle of Shadows 2 is full of fantasy, imagination and magic.

"You've ruined everything!" David screeched.

"...Now I'm the chosen one", Ryan shouted back. David looked upon his brother. His hair hung in long strands. His eyes surrounded by dark circles, starred intensely at him. David could sense his brother's power unlike ever before!

About the Author

Jesse VanDyke was born in Chapel Hill, NC. He grew up in Fearrington Village with two younger brothers. He lived there for 18 years before attending Liberty University, in Virginia, then Palm Beach Atlantic University in West Palm Beach, FL, where he met his wife Joy. Together they have a son, Tristan. They have been involved in education for over ten years, gaining their masters in education in school counseling from Florida Atlantic University. Jesse has taught elementary in South Florida for ten years and is now the Director of Academics at Bethany Christian School in Fort Lauderdale. When writing this series of books, Jesse, becomes like the musician James Taylor who is ***"Gone to Carolina in My Mind".***

For some additional reading on North Carolina, Chapel Hill and legends about Gimghoul Castle, check out these great websites.

http://carrboro.com/gimghoulcastle.html
http://gradschool.unc.edu/funding/gradschool/weiss/interesting_place/history/castle.html
http://raleightelegram.com/201210313653

www.ingramcontent.com/pod-product-compliance
Ingram Content Group UK Ltd.
Pitfield, Milton Keynes, MK11 3LW, UK
UKHW020221250726
13967UKWH00001B/117
9 781304 607041